ROCHESTER HILLS PUBLIC LIBRARY
500 OLDE TOWNE ROAD
ROCHESTER, MICHIGAN 48307

AUG 19 2002

JOURNEY TO THE PAST

ANCIENT EGYPT

Romano Solbiati

A Harcourt Company

Austin · New York
www.steck-vaughn.com

© Copyright 2001, text, Steck-Vaughn Company

© Copyright 1999 Istituto Geografico De Agostini, Novara

All rights reserved. No part of this book may be reproduced or utilized in any form or by any means, electronic or mechanical, including photocopying, recording, or by any information storage and retrieval system, without permission in writing from the Publisher. Inquiries should be addressed to: Copyright Permissions, Steck-Vaughn Company,
P.O. Box 26015, Austin, TX 78755

Published by Raintree Steck-Vaughn, an imprint of Steck-Vaughn Company

Library of Congress Cataloging-in-Publication Data

Solbiati, Romano.
   Ancient Egypt / Romano Solbiati.
     p. cm. — (Journey to the past)
   Includes index.
   ISBN 0-7398-1954-2
   1. Egypt—History—Nineteenth dynasty, ca. 1570–1320 A.D.—Juvenile literature. 2. Ramses II, King of Egypt—Juvenile literature. [1. Egypt—Civilization—To 332 B.C.]   I. Title.   II. Series.

DT88 .S63 2001
932'.014—dc21   **3 3158 00251 7115**   00-059210

Editorial Coordinator: Cristina Drago
Editor: Stefano Sibella
Translated by: Mary Stuttard

Illustrations: Aldo Ripamonti
Graphics: Marco Volpati

Raintree Steck-Vaughn Staff: Marion Bracken, Pam Wells
Project Manager: Lyda Guz
Photo Research: Claudette Landry, Sarah Fraser

Photo Credits:

P.48a ©Yann Arthus-Bertrand/CORBIS; p.48b ©Gian Berto Vanni/CORBIS; p.48c ©Roger Wood/CORBIS; p.48d ©Yann Arthus-Bertrand/CORBIS; p.49a ©Julian Calder/CORBIS; p.49b ©Richard T. Nowitz/CORBIS; p.49c ©Michael Nicholson/CORBIS; p.49d ©Farrell Grehan/CORBIS; p.50a ©Adam Woolfitt/CORBIS; pp.50b, 51b ©Roger Wood/CORBIS.

All other photographs are from the Archives of IGDA.

Printed in Italy

1 2 3 4 5 6 7 8 9 04 03 02 01

ROCHESTER HILLS PUBLIC LIBRARY
500 OLDE TOWNE ROAD
ROCHESTER, MICHIGAN 48307

AUG 19 2002

TABLE OF CONTENTS

Guidebook..2
   A Waterway to Thebes!...................4
   Welcome!...................................6
The Old City..12
   The Temple of Amon at Karnak...............12
   The Sanctuary at Luxor....................14
   The Royal Palace of Ramses II..............16
   The House of Life.........................18
Art and Architecture...........................20
   The Colossi of Memnon.....................20
   Deir el-Bahari............................22
The Wealthy Neighborhoods................24
   The Luxury Villa..........................24
The Working-Class Districts................26
   Deir el-Medina............................26
   The Farmers' Houses.......................28
The Market...30
   The Market at Elephantine.................30
Festivals and Ceremonies.....................32
   The Tribute at Memphis....................32
   The Festival of Opet......................34
   The Royal Jubilee at Pi Ramesse...........36
   The Mysteries of Abydos...................38
Trips Outside the City.........................38
   Tell el-Amarna............................40
   The Pyramids of Giza and the Sphinx.......42
   Abu Simbel................................44
The Armed Forces...............................46
   The Fortress of Buhen.....................46
Egypt Today.......................................48
Some Important Facts.........................52
Glossary..53
Further Reading.................................54
Index..55–56

Guidebook

A Waterway to Thebes

Would you like to visit Thebes? Well, the best way to reach the city is to travel along the Nile River. You can easily travel south driven by the fresh, northerly breeze. Going north is another story. It means hard work—all hands are needed on the oars!

Egypt is called the gift of the Nile, you know, but the Egyptians call the Nile a gift of Hapi, god of the flood. They believe that every year, usually between our months of July and September, Hapi sees that the Nile River overflows its banks. During the flooding the Nile becomes a vast lake, then a swamp. As the water recedes, the Nile deposits a thin layer of rich, dark soil called silt on the surrounding land. Lush fields appear as the silt enriches the soil for farming. The Egyptians have named the strip of

fertile land that borders the Nile *Kemet,* which means "black earth."

Tauri, meaning "Two Kingdoms," is another name that the Egyptians give their homeland. Again Hapi is involved. It is Hapi who sees that the Nile ties together the entire country as it carries the gift of water from its source in central Africa northward. The name Tauri is represented by the hieroglyph that means "to tie."

The Egyptians describe the Nile as a highway that carries goods and people along its course. They also describe the Nile as a flower. How is that possible? Just imagine the main stem of the flower as the river itself as it flows more than 6,000 kilometers from the south near the equator to the Mediterranean Sea known then as the Vast Green Water. The maze of waterways that fan out just above Memphis forms the petals. The flower's roots are planted in the interior of Africa.

Now Thebes awaits you. A boat is leaving from Memphis for Thebes. Prepare your sea legs! Enjoy your visit.

Principal Locations and Symbols in Egypt

Kemet — Black Earth, Egypt
Taui — Two Kingdoms, Egypt
Piramesse — Ramses' Palace
Iunu — The Columns of Heliopolis
Mennefer — The Lasting and Beautiful Memphis
Rosetau — The Avenue in Giza
Akhetaton — The Horizon of Aton, Tell el-Amarna
Abgiu — Abidos
Uaset — Thebes, the Powerful
Abu — Elephantine
Suenet — The Market, Aswan
Usermaatra — The Power and Cosmic Harmony of Ra, Abu Simbel
Buhen — Fortress

Guidebook

Welcome!

Your first impression on arriving in Thebes may be that you will never be able to find your way. How can you take in such a city at one glance? In one direction the city seems to fade into the sandy plateaus and pit-shaped areas of the Western Desert. In the other direction, Thebes is wedged between the soft rocky hills and deep valleys of the Eastern Desert. The famous landmark, the Temple of Amon at Karnak, will help you to get your bearings. So will the pyramidlike peaks overlooking the Theban necropolises, or cemeteries. Very soon you will realize that Thebes is a special city, very different from all other cities.

Actually there is not just one Thebes, but two—East Thebes and West Thebes separated by the Nile River. East Thebes on the east bank of the Nile is known as the city of the living. Here you will find the great temples of Karnak and Luxor, the administrative centers for the city and for business, and residential sections with their markets and other service areas.

West Thebes is on the west bank. It is called the city of the dead because of the presence of vast necropolises. The necropolises are for the royal families and the nobility. These burial places are named the Valley of the Kings and the Valley of the Queens. The funeral temples of the pharoahs are here, too.

You probably know that there are at least three old towns in Thebes. There are Karnak and Luxor to the east. The royal palace and the land belonging to Ramses' kingdom is to the west. There a town is formed from a network of canals where you will find a mixture of working-class and rural areas that have developed side by side without any rhyme or reason.

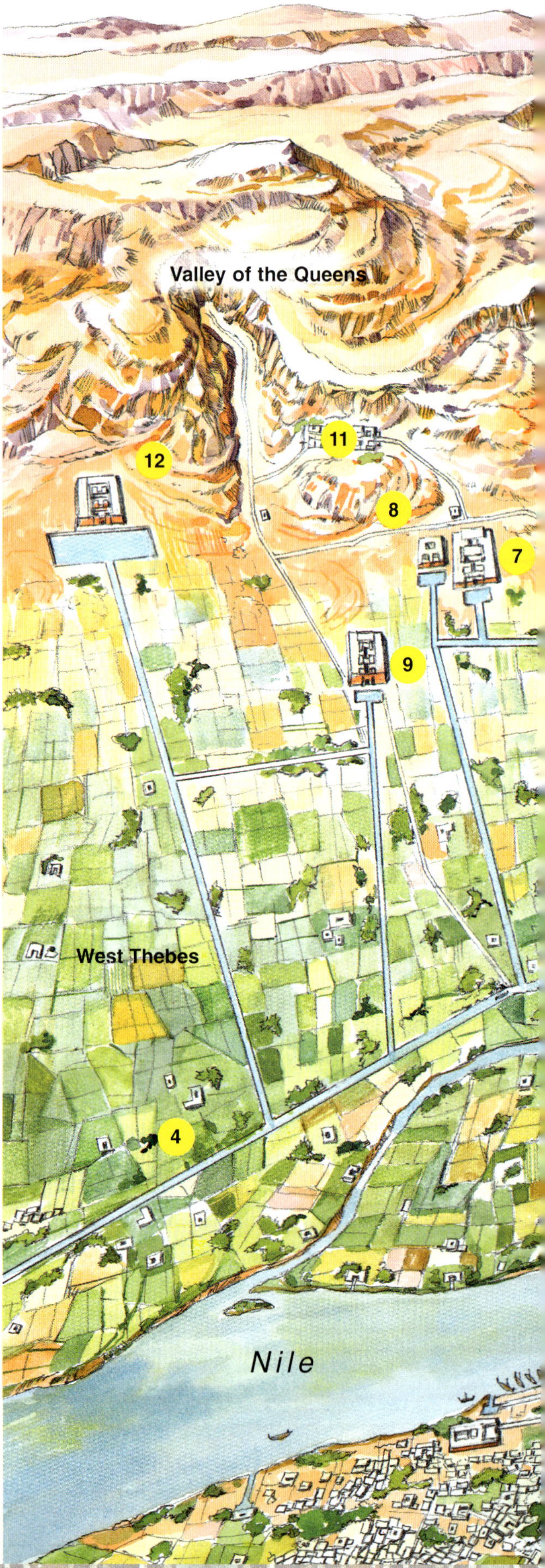

The Moral Capital

Thebes, Uaset in Egyptian, is called the queen of all cities, the eye of the creator, the center of the whole world. Thebans use superlatives when they talk about their city. Perhaps they exaggerate, but their pride is understandable.

Three centuries ago the national revolt against the barbaric Hittites, the first foreigners who ever dared to conquer Egypt, set out from Thebes. Since then, this sunkissed city has risen to become the capital of an empire spread across two continents, Africa and Asia.

Although the country's political capital is once again in Memphis in the north and the new royal palace is Pi Ramesse, the ancient city of Thebes retains its roles as the moral capital of the Two Kingdoms. The Theban temple of Amon is the principal religious center of all Egypt. The pharoahs come to Thebes to be crowned and buried, and Thebes is the most heavily populated and the richest city in all the empire!

1. The Temple of Amon-Re
2. The Temple of Montu
3. The Temple of Mut
4. Canal
5. The Temple of Seti I
6. The Temple of Thutmose III
7. The Pi Ramesse (Royal Palace) of Ramses II
8. The Temple of Thutmose IV
9. The Temple of Amenofis III (the Colossus of Memnon)
10. Deir el-Bahari
11. Deir el-Medina
12. The Palace of Amenofis III

7

Guidebook

Useful Information

What is the first thing you should do when you land in Thebes? Nothing! The scribes of the river police will take care of everything. You see, the Egyptian authorities have regulations full of red tape! Everything has to be checked, double-checked, and carefully registered, on papyrus of course.

Whatever you want to do, wherever you want to go, you have to find the right office, take along your papyrus, and wait for the scribe to fill out your request for authorization. That explains why in a country where less than one percent of the people can read, there are so many scribes.

This is not the only surprise that awaits you. A great number of the Theban monuments are temples, sacred places, or royal residences. All are closed to the public. To visit these places, you need special authorizations, which are given only in special circumstances, on papyrus with the state seal, issued by the offices of the vizier or one of the chief priests.

Not only is human law observed in Thebes, divine law is also observed. The Egyptians call this Ma'at, the law of universal order and harmony on earth imposed by the gods for humans to observe to the letter. The police and the courts take their work of carrying out the law very seriously. Every small violation of the law is severely punished. For a minor theft, at best you may get away with a fine, at worst you could be condemned to 100 blows with a stick. I dread to think what might happen to you if you committed a really serious crime such as violating a sacred building or a royal residence. If you exclude the death penalty, punishments range from having one of your hands, your tongue, nose, or ears cut off, to being sent to Nubia, a region south of Egypt.

Local Currency

Money as we understand it does not exist in Egypt. By law, all forms of payment, ranging from salaries to the purchase and sale of goods and services are paid in kind. For example, if you go to the market to buy, say, a pair of sandals, you need to take something attractive to give the shoemaker in exchange, something like an earring or a length of cloth.

What is more, you run the risk of wasting considerable time in exhausting bargaining before reaching a price that suits you both. To avoid this problem, the Egyptian state has decided to set prices in terms of certain metal weights. The deben, a copper weight of about 91 grams, is used to evaluate the average value of certain goods. If you want to buy a pair of sandals, for example, you will have to come up with one and one half deben or goods worth that amount. A sheep will cost you five deben, an ox 100 deben. However, the basic system of exchange in the Two Kingdoms remains bartering, or exchanging goods of equal value. So it is worth taking along precious objects, cloth, or incense with you. But remember, all trade in gold or silver is strictly controlled by the state.

Where to Find Food and Lodging

Egyptian hospitality is well-known. Given the continuous comings and goings of foreign merchants to and from Egypt, especially from Asia, you should have no trouble finding accommodations with a family almost anywhere, even with the more humble people.

When local festivals are celebrated, you are often allowed to stay in the guest rooms of temples or in the villas owned by the nobility. These are opened to welcome pilgrims on such occasions.

Finding something to eat is never a problem. You will see peddlers selling food on every street corner. Then there are the drinking houses. Here, in addition to finding a snack, you will also be able to play senet, an Egyptian board game, and stay up until the small hours of the morning listening to music or singing and dancing in company with the other customers.

The Egyptians do not use cutlery, so it is advisable, as well as good hygiene and good manners, to wash your hands and rinse your mouth before and after eating.

Addresses and Interesting Facts

Finding an address in Thebes can be a real challenge. The streets do not have names. The houses do not have numbers. And the streets often end at a wall or lead into a canal! But don't worry. The police are always ready to help people in difficulty, especially if they are foreigners. The scribes are helpful, too. They know everything about the city.

But be very careful how you ask for information. Never point your finger to indicate something. In Thebes pointing means you are casting the evil eye over someone. Avoid bringing your hands to your chest. To an Egyptian this means you think the person is stupid. The Egyptians believe that the heart is the center of a person's intelligence. Even if you are hungry, do not touch your stomach or your mouth. For the Egyptians the stomach is the center of magical powers and touching the mouth is a sign of hostility.

Just one more thing to remember! For the Egyptians, the Mediterranean Sea is always "behind" them, and the sources of the Nile are always "in front." Remember that when someone mentions the left bank and the right bank of the Nile River.

Dress

In Thebes you may very well experience torrid heat, so the local dress may suit you best. Egyptians wear simple clothes made of cotton or linen that is woven in such a way that the material becomes like a fine, almost transparent veil.

One garment still in fashion is a kind of short skirt. It is popular among the workers and the priests and is traditionally worn by the pharoahs. Apart from the countryside where people often go naked, the most common garment for both men and women everywhere is a tunic of calf- or ankle-length. Important officials and high-level workers wear several tunics in layers. A short cape of the same material is often worn over the tunics.

The wealthier classes often wear jewelry and elaborate wigs on top of which are placed cone-shaped vessels of perfumed ointment. Both sexes outline the eyes with kohl, or dark eye makeup. Kohl is also used to protect the skin from insect bites and from sunburn. Shoes, such as sandals made from papyrus, leather, or braided palm leaves, are considered a luxury.

A word of advice—avoid wearing the color blue unless you are going to a funeral. Here blue is the color of mourning.

What to do in the case of illness

People say Thebes enjoys a healthful climate because it is near the desert. This is true, but not completely. During the time of the Nile floods, the climate is sultry and suffocating. Clouds of small flies and mosquitoes fill the air.

The climate in the desert is really no joke either. By nightfall the cold can become intense. There also is the scorching wind that blows continuously for 50 days at a time to consider. And do not forget the scorpions, the cobras, the crocodiles, and the hippopotamuses that live in the desert.

However, there is some good news too. Egyptian medicine is extremely advanced, and Egyptian doctors are world-famous for their professional skills. There already exist in Egypt more than 80 different types of medical specialists, including oculists, dentists, cardiologists, surgeons, gynecologists, pediatricians, and ear, nose, and throat doctors. Two hundred types of illness are treated successfully.

In Thebes you can also count on the clinic and sanctuary of Deir el-Bahari, probably the best in the country. Many leading doctors work in the temples and military barracks there while others work in the Houses of Life along with several general practitioners. Because they know how to treat all types of illnesses, they are considered genuine masters of the art of medicine.

If all this is not enough, you can always ask at one of the Houses of Life to see someone who is considered an expert in magic. Magic is very highly regarded in the Two Kingdoms. It is considered the most important science of all as it involves the ability to manipulate supernatural forces. The pharaoh in person is thought be the most important magician in Egypt.

If you chose magic as a form of treatment, you will have to undergo seemingly incomprehensible but possibly effective rituals. In addition, you will be given a papyrus or a piece of ivory covered with magic formulas, together with mysterious potions and amulets.These should be used to exorcize, or drive out, demons and chase away any type of negative energy until your health is restored.

Guidebook

What can you eat in Thebes?

In the city of Thebes, you have a wide choice of food ranging from simple but appetizing local cuisine using traditional recipes to the elaborate cuisine of the wealthy. Although wealthy people have a wide choice of foods and use such spices and herbs as cumin, dill, cinnamon, sage, thyme, and rosemary, they share two main items with ordinary people—bread and beer.

Egyptian bread is delicious. It is made from wheat or *spelt* and is baked in a variety of forms—round, triangular, rectangular, conical, and even in the shape of people and animals. The beer made chiefly from barley is more or less strong and sweet, always fizzy and deliciously cool.

The diet of ordinary people is basically vegetarian. You should try their tasty breadcake filled with sweet onions and garlic or their original lentil salad boiled with lotus and papyrus shoots. A traditional fish is bulti, from the Nile. Bulti is often served dry or pickled, together with goat's cheese. Heartier meals include soups and purees made from cereals and vegetables such as lettuce, broad beans, cucumbers, leeks, and peas.

Wealthy Egyptians regularly eat meat dishes such as duck, lamb, oxen, and often wild game. The meat is boiled, roasted, or braised and served with aromatic sauces. Wealthy people enjoy grapes, dates, figs, melons, and watermelons, in addition to plums, walnuts, and pomegranates. You may enjoy Eygptian crackers coated with honey or carob syrup. Honey is nicknamed liquid gold or the tears of Ra.

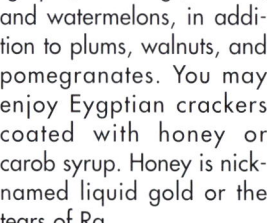

You will find wine in the homes of the wealthy. The wine is made from grapes grown in the Nile Delta or oases of the Western Desert or even in distant Syria.

The Nubian cuisine is definitely less varied. Nubians cook wild game such as antelope, gazelles, bear, cranes, and ostrich, over charcoal, and drink milk.

Now here is a piece of advice. Before you eat in the morning, adopt the habit of rinsing your mouth out with natron, or sodium salt. It is a local tradition and is also extremely hygienic. The Egyptians call breakfast "sen scem scem," which means "rinsing the mouth and the teeth."

Where to shop?

On condition that you have something to give in exchange, you can shop almost anywhere in Egypt. The best opportunities are during the numerous national or local festivals and holidays. Then the Egyptian cities transform themselves into noisy, colorful, open-air fairs and markets. You will find all kinds of goods set out on rush mats—foodstuffs, jewelry, leather goods, pottery, glass, and home furnishings. You'll see wooden boxes and chests for beauty products, palettes for kohl, and alabaster vases for ointments. There are toys, medicinal plants—the list is almost endless.

In the markets you can also find traveling barbers and wig sellers. They work in open booths and serve fresh drinks to their clients. Look carefully and you may find tatooers from Libya and Nubia although the Egyptian authorities consider tatooing a barbaric and vulgar practice.

In the Two Kingdoms it will be difficult to find expert craftsmen's workshops open to the public. These are usually part of the temples and the palaces of royalty and the wealthy. So, if you really want to visit these workshops—as you already know—you will have to obtain special permission.

Weights and Measures

The unit of weight currently used in Egypt at this time is the deben. It is equal to 91 grams and is divided into 10 parts. Bread is weighed by the loaf, which weighs between 28 and 33 ounces.

Liquids are measured by the jar, which is the equivalent of .13 of a gallon. Cereals are measured by the barrel, corresponding to nearly 1.1 gallon. Length is measured in royal cubits divided into 28 fingers, or the length of the arm from the end of the middle finger to the elbow. There is also a small cubit, used by architects and divided into 24 fingers.

Egyptians calculate distances in units of 20,000 cubits, which is the equivalent of 6.5 miles. They measure area in a unit equal to 100 square cubits, or 29,440 square feet.

Measuring Time: Hours and Calendars

The Egyptians have great respect for the rhythms of nature. Although they divide the day into 24 parts, the length of an hour in the daytime and nighttime varies depending on the time of year. Therefore, Egyptian clocks, that is, sundials and water clocks, are changed each season.

Egyptians use three different types of calendars. The first is an astronomical calendar based on the star called Sirius, which appears at the new year (around July 19). The second is a sacred calendar based on the phases of the moon and used by the priests to fix religious holidays. The third is a civil calendar based on the Nile floods. It is divided into three seasons—the floods from the end of July to the middle of November; the emersion of the land in the Nile flood waters, from mid-November to mid-March, when the planting takes place; and finally the dry season, from mid-March to mid-July, dedicated to harvesting the crops.

A civil year has 12 months of 30 days each, plus five days of passage to the new year. These five days are considered unlucky, since they fall outside the cycle of the seasons. A week is ten days long, with one day for rest and ancestor worship.

Children in Thebes

The Egyptians love children, whom they consider a gift from the gods. They usually have large families. Ramses II is said to have more than 150 children.

In Thebes, as throughout the Two Kingdoms, the population is extremely young. You will often see women breast-feeding their babies. Babies are commonly breast-fed until they are three. You will see boys and girls running around totally naked, their hair in the typical childhood braid. A lock of hair is wound into a curl and worn chiefly on the right side of the head, which is completely shaven.

Among the most popular toys are balls, tops, rag dolls, models of such animals as crocodiles and hippopotamuses, clay marbles, model carts, and pea shooters.

The end of childhood comes quite early, usually between 10 and 12 years. The transition from childhood to adulthood is marked for both sexes by the cutting of the childhood braid.

The Egyptians, What Curious People!

It is important that you remember two or three basic facts about the Egyptians. First, the Egyptians have an inborn sense of hierarchies. There is no other explanation for their ability to invent more than 2,000 titles for the nobility and the priestly classes and to create the huge number of administrative and military positions. Respect for these hierarchies together with a deep sense of moral honesty are the basic principals of the Egyptian civilization. Both are part of the Ma'at, or Rule, by which they live.

Egyptian society resembles an immense pyramid, with the pharaoh at the top, the majority of his subjects—mostly manual workers and farmers—at the bottom, and the nobles, military, scribes, priests, and craftsmen in the middle.

The second fact to bear in mind is the importance of religion or, more precisely, magic and religion which are closely connected in Egyptian society. Every aspect of Egyptian civilization is influenced or regulated by this combination. Everything revolves around the pharaoh, who is considered both king and god, and therefore the principal priest-magician in the land. So we can understand that the Egyptians, who consider themselves an integral part of a sacred civilization, have a certain sense of superiority toward foreigners.

But this is as far as it goes because the Egyptians also possess two extremely rare qualities: respect for and tolerance of others. This may be because many gods coexist in Egypt, together with the conviction that every human being possesses a soul. This is why, compared to other neighboring peoples, the Egyptians hold women in high regard. Women in Egypt are considered almost equal to men.

The idea that a human being may be bought and sold like an object is repulsive to the Egyptians. However, to be honest, since the Egyptians have extended their empire to Asia, slaves won in wars or sent to pay debts have also begun to appear in Egypt.

One final fact to remember. The Egyptians are extremely aware of personal hygiene.

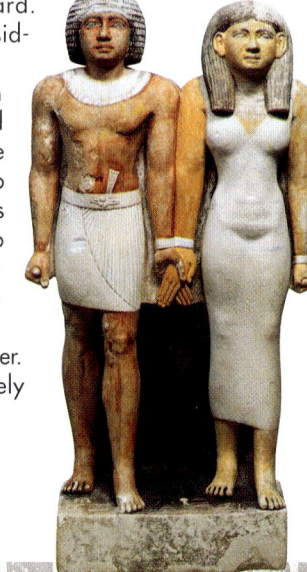

11

The Old City

The Temple of Amon at Karnak

To reach Karnak, you go along a canal lined with willow trees that connects the Nile with the landing-stage for the Temple of Amon, king of the gods. Karnak is the largest sacred area in all Egypt. The Temple of Amon alone covers an area of 60 acres. More than 80,000 people, including priests, craftsmen, and farmers, work there. It oversees about 70 villages, which have more than a half million head of cattle. Its fleet consists of more than 80 ships.

The temple itself is extremely impressive. The outer walls are as high and as thick as those of a fortress. Only the golden tops of its obelisks that reflect the sun's rays skyward and the pillar towers at either side of the entrance arch are higher than the walls.

You approach the main entrance along a wide avenue lined with sphinxes. Passing through the entrance, you find yourself in the famous hypostyle, or main room, of the

THE SACRED LAKE

The Ancient Egyptians believed that at the dawn of time, before every other thing, before the sky, before the light, even before the gods, the only thing that existed was an ocean of energy. Then creation began. The sun appeared in the sky, and the ocean of energy was driven back to the edge of the world. The first gods were born, and from the celestial ocean flowed the waters out of which rose the hill that gave Earth its beginning. Hapi, god of the Nile, rose, too. They believe that water has continued to gush from that ocean, creating the spring water that feeds the sacred lake in Karnak, their symbol of creation.

temple. The roof of this room is made from decorated cedar wood and is supported by rows of huge multicolored columns. The floor is made of a natural alloy of gold and silver. The room is half-lit, filled with the heavy smell of incense, and communicates a strong sense of the sacred and powerful.

The rest of the temple is a labyrinth of doorways, courtyards, statues, colonnades, chapels, and all kinds of buildings in various shapes and sizes. In an enclosure, farther inside the temple, there is a huge sacred lake where the dawn rituals are celebrated and where holy water is drawn to be used in the services held in the temple.

An interesting fact: a rare perfume called "the perfume of the gods" is produced in the laboratories in Karnak. The perfume is distilled from 16 oils from all over the world.

Amon and the Theban Triad

The Egyptians identify Amon as the hidden god, the creator, but also "he who makes all things possible and he who protects us." Amon sometimes appears in human form and sometimes with the head of a ram, the animal sacred to him. He is often identified with Ra, the sun god and husband of Mut, the "mother" of all mothers. Khonsu, god of the moon, is Amon's son. These three gods form the Theban Triad; each one has a temple in Karnak.

THE OLD CITY

The Sanctuary of Luxor

Luxor is the throbbing center of Thebes. It is the hub of all state and local government for the whole of Upper Egypt. The vizier of southern Egypt resides here, as does the local mayor. The tax offices are based here, the arsenals, military barracks, courthouses, factories, state storehouses, customs offices, and so on. Each provides work for the bands of scribes we often see here in Egypt.

Luxor is a noisy, bustling city, too. It has a thriving port, with a constant flow of cargo boats and pleasure craft arriving from north or south together with those used for operating the local river traffic. Like every port, it offers street markets, taverns, and many types of entertainment.

Along the riverbanks you will see groups of expensive houses owned by the local civil servants, nobles, and merchants, all closely watched by armed guards. Beyond are areas of crowded, noisy, working-class neighborhoods, including the quarters where the local craftsmen have their workshops that open directly onto the streets. Farther away from the river are the farms and villas belonging to the aristocracy.

The Temple of Amon is set apart from all the rest. It is as impressive as the Temple of Karnak. The two temples are connected by a wide avenue more than 2 miles long. The Temple of Amon is generally considered to be a less important seat of Amon. But in actual fact the celebrations marking the New Year, during the time of the Nile floods, are held in the most secret part of the temple. This sacred rite is called *hierogami*, which means the marriage of the pharaoh with his chief royal wife.

Mut, the Great Mother
Mut, the wife of Amon and mother of the moon god Khonsu, has a thousand forms and faces. In Luxor she is the mother of the pharaoh and his chief royal wife. She is Amonet, too, the lover of Amon. Like Hathor, the goddess of the cow's horns, Mut is the symbol of fertility and of love. However, she is also the reverse of all the above. In hieroglyphics her name is symbolized by a vulture, and the Egyptian word mut *means "death." When she appears as Sekhmet, the lioness god, who drinks from the sacred waters of her temple in Karnak, Mut is the destroyer of all the enemies of Ma'at. She is the goddess of order and justice.*

Ka: man and his double

Akh, ba, ka—according to the Egyptians, these are our souls. The most important is ka, something like our "double." *Ka* represents our combined physical and mental energies, which our body loses in death and which it must regain in the afterlife in order to become immortal. The *ka* was believed to be regenerated each year at the time of the annual floods.

15

THE OLD CITY

The Royal Palace of Ramses II

The Royal Palace of Ramses II in Thebes is part of the great, sacred fortress built by and named after the king, in West Thebes. The choice of location, on the edge of the desert, among the royal funeral temples, is, in itself, a statement of the distance between the pharaoh and the rest of the world.

Do not think for one moment that you will be allowed to enter the palace! You will only be allowed to see it from the outside. Simply join those invited to an official awards ceremony for the highest dignitaries in the kingdom, an event held periodically at the Royal Palace. The rite takes place in an area just outside the palace, a place that is spectacular in itself.

The palace entrance is dominated by two colossal, awe-inspiring statues of the pharaoh, in black granite. Showing little emotion, the soldiers from the royal guard line the access staircase and the courtyard where the ceremonies are held.

The most thrilling moment is when the king comes to the edge of a raised loggia, his chief wife beside him, followed by two ritualist priests. This loggia is called "the window of appearances" and is supposed to protect mere mortals from direct contact with the divine energy of the pharaoh, which is said to have the power to strike them dead.

As a herald announces the names of the award winners, the king throws the prizes into the court. You will see necklaces, bracelets, and occasionally the highly prized military decoration of the three golden flies, symbol of the highest rank in the army.

The Pharaoh's Crowns

For the Egyptians everything about a pharaoh is supernatural in nature and expresses an irresistible magical power. This extends even to his clothes and accessories too, for example his sandals, which may be touched only by specially chosen priests. The same is true for the royal insignia: the scepters, the false beard, the bull's tail tied to his girdle, and above all his crowns. The crowns are believed to contain living forces, that is to say, to have energy of their own. So the double crown, which unites the red crown of Lower Egypt with the white crown of Upper Egypt, not only represents the unity of the kingdom, but also protects it. It is the same for the blue crown. It reaffirms the celestial and sacred origins of the monarch; it also serves to scatter his enemies in war.

The Old City

The House of Life

The House of Life is an institution you will find only in Egypt. The most important branches in Thebes are those in the Temple of Amon in Karnak and the one annexed to the royal palace of Ramses II. The House of Life is a school, an academy, and a cultural center all rolled into one. Here the best brains in the country study, do research, and work. All kinds of people gather at this center of learning—theologians, diplomats, historians, geographers, astronomers, mathematicians, architects, doctors, and pharmacists. Healers, too, as well as astrologers, and magicians study and train here.

Such a varied mixture of disciplines is further evidence of the special nature of Egyptian culture where science, religion, and magic are so closely bound together.

The institution has well-equipped laboratories and astronomical observatories. It is a well-organized institution, with a president, a senior lecturer, and a chief scribe.

The institution acts as a publishing center, too. The most important Egyptian literary and scientific texts are copied, annotated, and restored here. School textbooks are written here and calendars are drawn up.

The most important Egyptian documents are stored in the library in The House of Life. Here you will find the documents that contain information about all the Egyptian magical practices: *The Book of the Dead, The Texts of the Pyramids,* and *The List of Favorable and Unfavorable Days.*

Ears on the Back
Basic instruction also takes place in the House of Life. The teaching equipment is simple: a straw and pieces of broken pots to write on (Papyrus is too precious!), and a whip in the hands of the master. An old Egyptian saying is: "A boy's ears are on his back."

18

THE POWER OF AMULETS

In the most secret rooms of the House of Life, a few especially chosen people are taught the mysterious practices of magic such as the preparation of amulets, or charms. The effectiveness of the amulets depends on the materials from which they are made—chiefly lapis lazuli, turquoise, carnelian, gold—and on the energy with which they are charged.

Amulets sell like hot cakes in Egypt. You too can have an amulet provided you know what it symbolizes and what to do with it. So if you need strength, choose a heart or an ankh, the cross of life. For good health choose the knot of Isis or a special ring that guarantees long life. Another popular amulet is the scarab with its image of a beetle, the symbol of change.

Thoth and the sacred language

"Writing of the gods" is the name given to hieroglyphics, which by definition are sacred symbols. They may be written in the temples, in the tombs, and in what the Egyptians call books, but they are not publicly circulated simply because they are the words of the gods. This rule is so strictly observed that all Egyptian diplomatic correspondence is written in other languages or in a cursive form of Egyptian script.

Thoth, the god of knowledge and magic, is the patron of sacred language. Sometimes he appears as an ibis. At other times, he is more threatening as a baboon. The Egyptians believe that Thoth invented the hieroglyphs and guards their deepest secrets, which he shares only with the pharaoh.

Art and Architecture

The Colossi of Memnon

If you stay in Thebes, you simply have to see the Colossi of Memnon. To admire them, you will have to ferry across to West Thebes and then travel on by boat or mule. It will take you a whole day, but it is really worthwhile. Even seen from a distance, the two sandstone giants will amaze you. They seem to be gazing beyond the horizon into eternity.

There is a legend about this place that was started by the Greeks. The legend claims that the colossi are not just ordinary statues but the incarnation of Memnon, the mythical Ethiopian king killed by Achilles during the Trojan Wars. This is the origin of their names. In fact, the statues represent one of the most famous pharaohs of all time, Amenhotep III, and are mounted on the pillars either side of the entrance to his funeral temple.

Despite its origins as a funeral temple, there is nothing gloomy or sad about this palace. It has a series of double-ribboned white and blue royal flags, fluttering in the wind. The temple facade shows scenes from life pictured with elegance and refinement. The throned statues of the pharaoh transmit a strong sense of kindness.

Each morning the gilded bronze entrance gates of the temple open wide to greet the dawn and remain open until sunset. All day the temple teems with people. It is a pity that recently there has been a rumor that Ramses II intends to dismantle the temple of his predecessor to finish his own. Well, a god can do whatever he wishes, I suppose!

A World Apart

West Thebes is the kingdom of the "dwellings for a thousand years," in other words, the funeral temples of the great pharaohs and the priests in their service. The word "service" is well-chosen because *priest* in Egyptian means "a divine servant." It is a good choice because the role of a priest is to look after or attend the gods with offerings, rituals, and prayers.

The priests are a closed caste. The office is hereditary. You will recognize priests immediately because all their bodily hair has been removed, including their eyebrows and eyelashes. This is a sign of purity. The priests who perform rituals are in a special category, recognizable by their leopard-skin cloaks.

The Divine Room of Anubis

Along the canals of West Thebes, you will occasionally find an isolated brick or stone building protected from the eyes of the outside world by high walls. This is certainly "a pure place," which describes the special workshop where the age-old art of embalming the dead is practiced.

The building is dedicated to Anubis, the god with the head of a jackal. He is believed to be the protector of the dead and to have first applied the technique of embalming to the body of the god Osiris. Since then, the preparation of a mummy, which can require up to 70 days' work, is performed under the supervision of a specialized priest who just happens to wear the mask of Anubis.

Art and Architecture

Deir el-Bahari

Here is the wonder of wonders of West Thebes! A flight of steps leading up to the sky! There is a long avenue, two ramps of steps leading to the entrance, three wide terraces, and the kinds of hanging arcades where light and shadows merge. Beyond is the kingdom of the dead, the forbidden city of the Valley of the Kings.

But there is nothing here that reminds us of death. Even though this is the funeral temple of Queen Hatshepsut, a great pharaoh, everything here is a hymn of praise to life. That is precisely what she wanted the temple to be—a place of meditation for the spirit and recreation of the body and soul—a sort of clinic and sanctuary combined. Not only can you find the best doctors and healers here, you can also find those rare priests who are able to interpret dreams and draw up your horoscope. You will leave with new self-knowledge.

You can even find that rarest of plants, the incense tree, here. The garden of this temple is the only place in Egypt where the incense tree grows. By order of Hatshepsut, the great architect Senmut, who designed the temple of Deir el-Bahari, brought 30 young plants from the distant, legendary country of Punt. Punt is beyond Nubia, a region to the south, famed for its perfumed plants.

The story goes that between the queen and her architect there was a perfect understanding, perhaps even a great love story. An old wives' tale? Maybe so. However, the cartouche, the figure holding the hierglyphics of the name of Hatshepsut has been removed from the temple by the kings who followed her. But the nickname by which Deir el-Bahari is known still remains "Hatshepsut's smile."

THE SILENT MOUNTAIN PEAK
The gorge of Deir el-Bahari ends in a rocky barrier. Behind that is the Valley of the Kings. In the background looms a massive, pyramid-shaped rock called the Western Peak. The Thebans refer to it respectfully and fearfully as "The Peak," because for them it is the home of the cobra goddess Merseger, the goddess of silence, the jealous guardian of the royal necropolises.

The Fields of Ialu

Some people compare the avenue leading to Deir el-Bahari with the Egyptian version of heaven, that is, the Fields of Ialu. Here the blessed dead, carried across the pools and along the canals by the Boat of the Sun, spend their time feasting and resting in the shade of a garden that is eternally green. In fact, after you pass the two lions flanking the entrance to the temple of Hatshepsut, you walk between two rows of sphinxes. A variety of plants, such as palms and incense trees, grows beside the two rows. It is a real oasis!

Two artificial lakes are almost hidden by the lush vegetation. Situated on either side of the avenue, each lake is decorated with clumps of papyrus and lotus flowers. They are home to many species of birds and fish. It is a wonderful place where you can rock gently in a boat, just as you would in the Fields of Ialu.

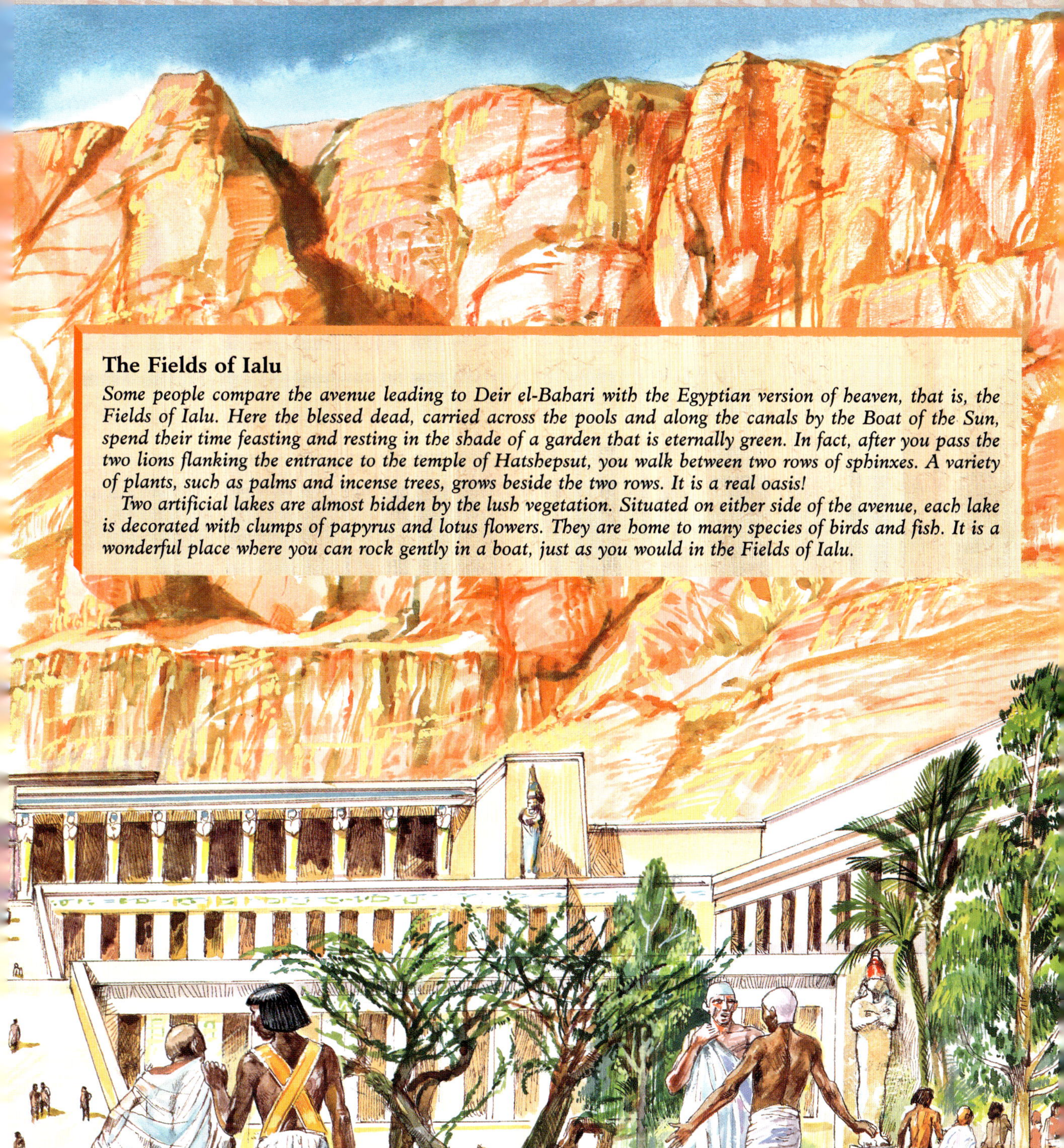

THE WEALTHY NEIGHBORHOODS

The Luxury Villa

Walking along the riverbanks of East Thebes or along the avenue that connects Karnak with Luxor, you will often find walled gardens with guards on duty at the entrance. They protect the villas belonging to the Theban ruling classes: nobles, notables, and dignitaries.

Some of the buildings are several stories high; others are on one level and extend into the surrounding countryside. They all follow the same model. They are totally self-sufficient, economically speaking, and are built in such a way as to separate all the household service areas, such as stables, storerooms, kitchens, craftsmen's workshops, and servants' quarters from the owner's residence.

Guest rooms include bedrooms, dressing rooms, toilet facilities, a dining room, and reception rooms. The entire residence has polished stone floors, valuable wooden furniture, and brightly painted walls decorated with natural or geometric motifs, or patterns.

The chief attraction in the house is the garden. It is a charming place of rest, with a pool in the center for swimming and fishing. It is surrounded by palm trees, ornamental shrubs and fruit trees, arbors and flower beds that attract birds. The garden is designed to create an area of welcome shade that is delightful to look at and full of delicious aromas.

If you are lucky enough to be invited to a reception at a villa like this, you will be treated like royalty. Maidservants will welcome you with garlands of flowers, and, if you wish, a servant will guide you to a hot steam bath. Then you will be given a refreshing shower and massaged with invigorating oils. Afterward, wearing suitable clothes and the required Egyptian wig topped with a cone of perfumed ointment, you will be accompanied to the banquet. Now you can eat, drink, and enjoy music, dancing, games, and conversation until dawn!

Bastet, the cat goddess
The Egyptians have always worshiped the cat, which they claim is the first animal to be domesticated. They honor the cat in the form of Bastet, goddess of joy, and daughter of Ra, the sun god. In the houses of all social classes, cats live freely and totally undisturbed.

THE RHYTHM OF THE DANCE: THE KHEBAIT DANCERS
No reception held in Thebes is considered complete without music and dance. But an orchestra, even one with several instruments such as the harp, lute, flute, castanets, and percussion to accompany a fine singer is not quite enough. You have to have the Khebait dancers. They are acrobatic dancers who are trained to interpret sounds, forms, colors, and gestures through their graceful movements. You know, in Egypt, dancing, singing, and music are one and the same thing.

The Working-Class Districts

Deir el-Medina

The village of Deir el-Medina is on the outskirts of Thebes. To reach the village, you have to cross the cultivated land of West Thebes, then start to climb up the first barren heights of the desert. But that is not all. Along the road your identity and destination will be checked frequently. Armed patrols will stop you at almost every step.

The reason for this is simple. First, the village belongs to the pharaoh. Second, the workers who live there are quite special because they are working on the necropolises of the Theban kings, including the sarcophagi, or stone coffins, and the decorations. Even the name of the place sounds important. It is known as "the residence of the servants of the seat of truth."

Actually, Deir el-Medina is a kind of artists' quarter. Here the best craftsmen from all over the Two Kingdoms come to work. They include sculptors, painters, potters, carpenters, glassblowers, jewelers, and cabinetmakers. The village is quite picturesque. It has small white houses with courtyards. The houses are quite similar, clean and well-kept. The straight roads are dotted with green palms, which offer a pleasant contrast with the ocher-brown colors of the mountain. There is the occasional water tank. You will also find a school, a clinic, a courthouse, and—too many guards! Except for produce from a few vegetable gardens and some stable animals, all the supplies are brought in from outside.

The community respects people's freedom, yet it has a military atmosphere that the workers of Deir el-Medina are used to. Many belong to a brotherhood of master craftsmen initiated into the secret of the symbols and are devoted to the cult of the living god, the pharaoh.

Usciabti
You might think that people buy the figures above as gifts. But that is not the case. The figures are statuettes of servants made from painted wood or colored pottery. They are used in the funeral rites. *Usciabti* are placed in a tomb to do the daily chores that the dead person might be required to do in the afterlife.

The artist and the gift of life

No one may be buried in Egypt unless his or her mummy has been reanimated during a special ceremony called the ceremony of the opening the mouth. In reality, the ears, nose, and eyes are "opened," too. This rule is also applied to statues, portraits, and sarcophagi, or stone coffins.

However, there is one small difference. Statues, portraits, and sarcophagi are reanimated twice. This is because the artist who has created the work—whether a sculptor, engraver or painter—is called sanki in Egypt. Sanki means "he who gives life."

27

THE WORKING-CLASS DISTRICTS

The Farmers' Houses

The Theban countryside is among the richest in the Nile Valley. Because of widespread irrigation and the hot climate, the farmers raise two harvests a year. Despite this, here as elsewhere in the Nile Valley, farmers have a very low standard of living. Why? Egyptian land belongs to the state, and more than half the farmers' earnings is lost in taxes. So, the little that remains is barely enough to feed families with six or seven children.

If you are invited to a farmer's house, do not be too surprised to find very few comforts. Apart from the granaries, shelter for the animals, and storehouses for tools, the living space may be only one whitewashed room with a floor of packed earth. The family meet here and spread out their rush mats on the floor to sleep, even on the coldest nights. There are few furnishings and few household objects. You will find

The Shaduf and the Baboons
These are two typical features of the Egyptian countryside. The shaduf is a simple but ingenious wooden balance that enables the farmers to pour water from one canal to another with little effort. Trained baboons are used by the farmers for picking fruit and to guard the farms.

water vases, saucepans, terra-cotta bowls, wooden spoons, and perhaps one or two wicker baskets.

The openings in the walls allow the light to enter together with the fresh north wind and serve as a barrier to the scorching desert wind. There is little else. On the threshing floor is a grindstone and an oven. The roof is flat and protected by a parapet, or low railing, and a cane trellis. On the floor is a terra-cotta stove for cooking and more rush mats where the family sits to eat, or even sleep during the hot season. The toilet facilities leave much to be desired. In the countryside, as in the city, garbage and everything else ends up in the canals that flow into the Nile.

Sekhmet and the Ibises

In high summer, when the harvest season is over and the new year marked by the Nile floods has not yet arrived, the *epagomeni* come. These are the five days that fall outside the regular Egyptian calendar. The farmers' lives seem to stand still.

The Egyptians believe these are the days when Sekhmet, the terrible goddess with the head of a lion, spreads sickness and disaster. Then suddenly flocks of white ibises appear from the south. The Egyptians believe that ibises are the incarnation of the wise and good god Thoth. The ibises herald the flood, and the parched countryside returns to life again.

THE MARKET

The Market at Elephantine

The island of Elephantine is an enchanting place. The final eddies of the First Cataract break against its banks. A city stands on the southernmost tip of the island. The center of the city is a fertile palm grove, but the city ramparts give it the air of a warship. Here you are at the frontier of the Two Kingdoms. Over there, beyond the roar of the rapids, is Nubia, the "corridor" to Africa.

Elephantine is the first province of Upper Egypt. With a favorable wind, you can sail up the Nile from Thebes and reach the island in four or five days. The trip is well worth the effort not only for the wild beauty of the landscapes you pass but also because Elephantine enjoys the special privilege of being in a duty-free zone, so there are no sales taxes.

This is why, over the years, an extraordinary market has flourished on the east bank of the Nile, just opposite the island of Elephantine. It is Aswan, which in Egyptian means "trade." In Aswan you can buy the best goods from three continents at very low prices. Take your pick of elephant tusks. (The elephant is the symbol of Elephantine.) and other more or less exotic African products such as leopard and giraffe skins, ostrich feathers, incense, ebony, and gold. There are semiprecious stones from Arabia and Central Asia—lapis lazuli, turquoise, and carnelian. There are elegant textiles and precious objects from Egypt, Asia, and the Mediterranean islands.

Here is a curious fact. In the desert not far from Aswan, you can see the biggest obelisk in the world, which is almost 80 royal cubits (about 140 feet) long! Unfortunately the obelisk cracked as it was being extracted from the quarry and has laid there unfinished ever since.

Khnum and the Potter's Wheel

According to Egyptian beliefs, Khnum is the god who protects Elephantine. Like the god Amon of Thebes, he has a human body and the head of a ram but with horizontal horns. Like Amon he is also considered to be a creator.

People say Khnum molded man from the mud deposited during the Nile floods and modeled him on a potter's wheel. This is why he is considered the patron god of potters, too. People also say that Khnum regulates the flow of the Nile by pressing on the waters with the soles of his sandals.

The Nilometer

In Elephantine's main temple, you will find Egypt's most important nilometer. The nilometer, which takes the form of a staircase with 90 steps descending into the Nile, allows experts to measure the level of water in the river. From ancient times, year after year, the priests indicate by notches the different heights reached by the Nile floods. They also add details to indicate whether the floods were beneficial or disastrous. Since the floods reach Elephantine about 20 days before they reach Thebes, this system of measurement allows the authorities of the Two Kingdoms to prepare for an even distribution of water throughout their country.

31

FESTIVALS AND CEREMONIES

The Tribute at Memphis

Would you like to witness a really outstanding event? Then find a way to visit Memphis for the ritual of the offering of gifts to the pharaoh by the foreign ambassadors to Egypt. This ceremony takes place each year in the second month of the sowing season and is followed by two days of celebrations. In the absence of the pharaoh, the vizier of the North often presides over the ceremony. A special area is decorated for the occasion, where the largest of the gifts such as elephants, Asian bears, giraffes, lions, and other wild African beasts may be received.

The members of the diplomatic corps are the most surprising and spectacular part of the ceremony. The Egyptian authorities will sit in front of a golden canopy to review the parade of the diplomatic representatives who will each lie flat before the pharaoh as a sign of respect. You will see Bedouin chiefs dressed in rough woolen tunics; Libyan kings wearing long cloaks and ostrich feathers in their curly hair, their skin decorated with tatoos; beardless Aegean princes wearing their hair in long braids, elegantly dressed in short skirts and sandals with raised tips; Asian nobles with pointed or combed beards, their heads swathed in multicolored square scarves, their torsos covered in various styles of clothes; and finally, the proud Nubian chieftains in their red wigs, brightly colored tunics and cloaks, and typical gold earrings. What an extraordinary sight!

The Long Arm of Ma'at

In Egypt there is a popular saying: *The pharaoh is like the sun, he makes Ma'at shine; the vizier is like the moon, he makes Ma'at count. Ma'at, always Ma'at, the Rule, the Law, the Justice!*

However, you need to appreciate that Ma'at is not an abstract idea. It is the sum total of age-old traditions and customs that together guarantee the stability of Egypt. Look carefully and you will see a small, gold amulet shining on the vizier's chest. It is the figure of a crouching woman, holding the ankh, the symbol of life, in one hand and wearing a feather in her hair. In the afterlife, the Egyptians believe the feather will be used to weigh the good and bad actions of each individual. In this life the vizier can weigh a person's actions and judge them.

MEMPHIS, THE WEIGHING SCALES OF THE TWO KINGDOMS

The city of Memphis is really old. It was founded by Menes, the first pharaoh, more than 1,800 years ago. It was once called the white wall after its fortified walls. Now it is called *Mennefer,* which means "lasting and beautiful." Memphis is always truly beautiful with its atmosphere of a huge, bustling port city.

Memphis has another name—*the weighing scales of the Two Kingdoms*—because it is situated where the Nile Delta and the Nile Valley join. The patron of Memphis is the mummy god Ptah, the protector of craftsmen. He is said to guard the secret of creation, having brought the world to life with a single word.

Egypt: The Temple of Ka Ptah

There is a strange rumor about the origins of the name *Egypt.* It seems to have come from the name of a great temple dedicated to the god Ptah in Memphis, which in Egyptian is "hut ka Pta." The Greeks seem to have interpreted the name in their own way, coming up with the name "Aigyptos," and confusing it with the name of the country.

33

FESTIVALS AND CEREMONIES

The Festival of Opet

The Festival of Opet begins a month and a half after the start of the new year, at the height of the Nile floods, when the weather is at its most sultry. Luckily you will not have to leave Thebes in order to enjoy the festival. The celebrations last about two weeks.

Opet is both a sacred and secular holiday. The sacred part centers on the ceremony in which the gods of the Theban triangle—Amon, Mut, and Khonsu—are taken by boat from Karnak to Luxor, where special rites to ensure a fertile agricultural year are performed. At the end of the festival, the statues are taken back again to Karnak by river.

The secular part is the happy, noisy merry-making that continues throughout the holiday. There are parades where people put on fancy clothes and sing and dance through the streets. There are street markets, acrobatic displays, sports competitions, such as foot races and wrestling with sticks Egyptian style, and as much food and beer as you want.

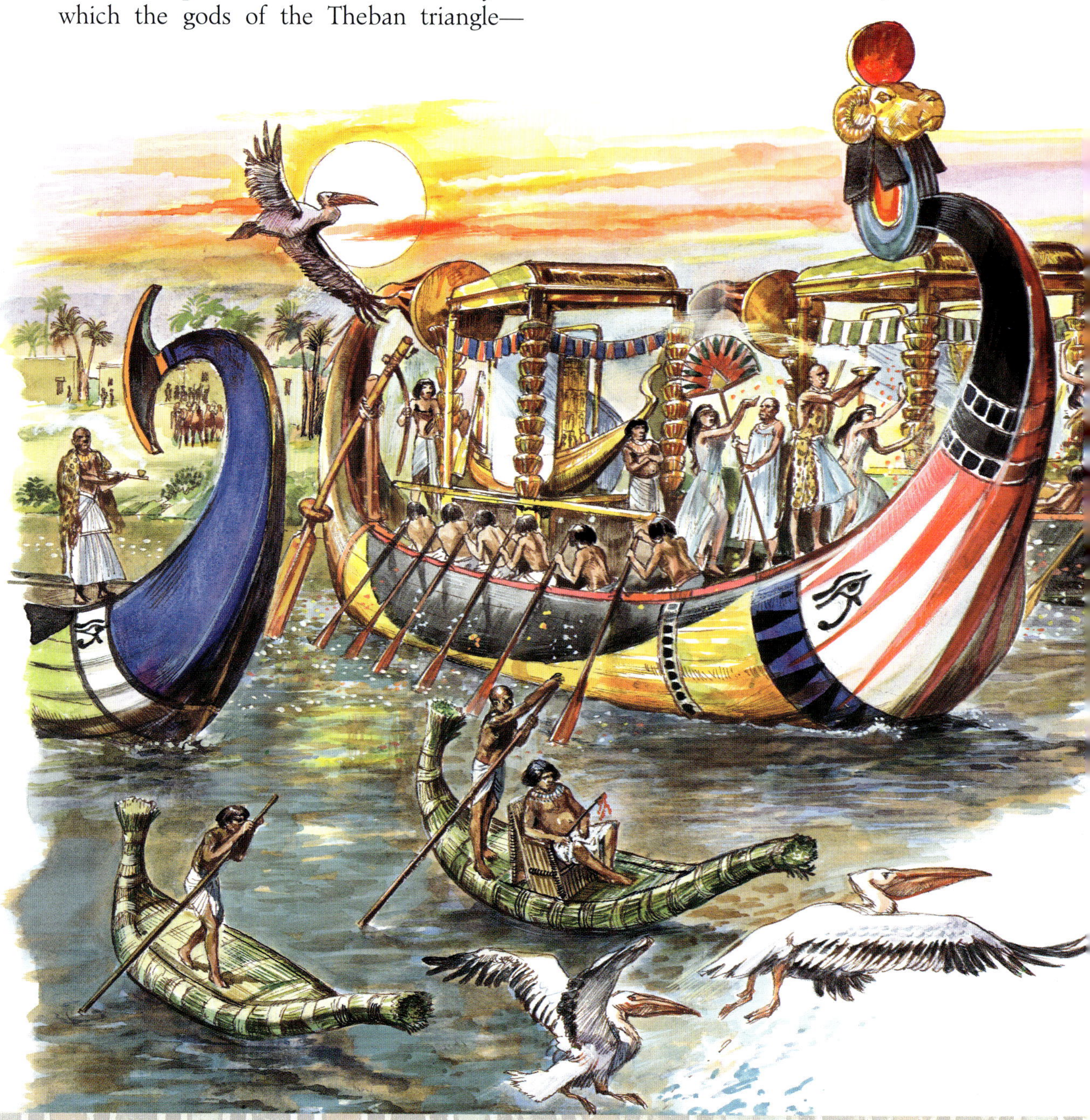

34

You simply must not miss the start of the festival, when the doors of the sanctuary at Karnak open to allow the pharaoh to pass through. The god king heads the procession of priests who carry on their shoulders the tabernacles, or shrines, that hold the sacred boats of the Triad as far as the wharf, where they are loaded onto the ships heading for Luxor.

Admire the beauty and elegance of the ships, especially the one that the god Amon and the pharaoh will board. Look very carefully at the procession before the pharaoh embarks. You may well spot a sacred boat swaying from time to time above the crowd! This means that the god of the boat has been asked for an oracle, or consultation. If the boat bends forward, the reply is positive; if it stops or draws back, it is negative. This event is held at dawn, so you had better get up early to enjoy it.

The Boat of the Sun and the Sacred Boats

For the Egyptians there is no better means of transportation than the boat. After all, the sun god Ra crosses the heavens in a boat, doesn't he? The long, nightly voyage of the stars and that of the souls in the afterlife take place in a boat. So it is not surprising that the statues of the gods are placed in boat-shaped tabernacles and transported from one temple to another along the Nile. Nor is it a surprise to find a sacred boat—sometimes as big as a real vessel—among the decorations of the gods' temples or the pharaoh's possessions.

In the Heart of the Temple

It is still night, but there is already excited activity inside the Temple of Amon at Karnak. The seals of the tabernacles where Amon, Mut, and Khonsu have spent the night have been broken and offerings are made to them. In the courtyard priests sing hymns to greet the morning. In the half-light of the temple, spirals of incense rise. The statues of the Theban Triad are washed, perfumed, and richly decorated. The pharaoh, who is leading the ceremony, gives the sign to proceed. Now each statue is placed at the center of its own wooden sacred boat and covered with a veil. Four men lift up each boat. It is dawn and the festival of Opet can begin.

FESTIVALS AND CEREMONIES

The Royal Jubilee at Pi Ramesse

If you are lucky enough to be in Egypt when Ramses II celebrates his jubilee in Pi Ramesse, his new capital, do not miss the opportunity to witness such a rare event. Unfortunately the public is barred from many parts of the ceremony. The rite is sacred, but it is enough to be nearby to feel a real sense of magic in the air.

The ceremony is a ritual performed to renew the Pharaoh's life force, exhausted after many years spent ruling the country. It is also a reaffirmation of the divine nature of the king and of his right to continue to govern the Two Kingdoms. The Egyptians call the event the festival of the bull's tail—the bull's tail being both a symbol of power and an attribute of gods and kings.

The jubilee lasts several days. The climax of the celebrations comes when Ramses II, dressed in the kind of clothing worn by the first kings of Egypt, runs eight times around the sacred perimeter, or edge, of the chapels dedicated to the chief gods of the nation. He covers four laps wearing the red crown of Lower Egypt and four laps wearing the white crown of Upper Egypt. At the center of this sacred area stands a *ged*, or pillar, that for the Egyptians is the symbol of stability and endless continuity.

During this ceremony, Ramses II holds a swallow-tailed scepter in his left hand, on which his royal rights are based. In his right hand, he holds an oar-shaped rudder that represents the king's ability to continue to govern the nation. At the end of the ceremony, the monarch shoots four arrows, one to the north, the others to the south, east, and west, to reconfirm his authority over the earth, the heavens, and the underworld, or afterlife.

Pi Ramesse, the Turquoise City

Ramses II has created a new city. It is called Pi Ramesse, which means "the kingdom of Ramses." Ramses chose to build the city exactly there—in the Nile Delta, looking toward Sinai, the gateway to Asia and the new horizons of the empire. Pi Ramesse is a garden city without walls. It is a promising port crisscrossed by numerous canals. The proximity of Sinai is evident from the facades of all the main buildings, which have been covered in turquoise, the precious stone from Sinai, sacred to Harthor, the goddess of love.

THE MAGIC OF THE HEART AND THE MONSTER APOPHIS

During the secret jubilee rituals, Ramses II wears the special amulet, usually given to the mummies, that the Egyptians believe helps dead people to overcome the terrible trials waiting for them in the underworld. This amulet is supposed to allow the Pharaoh to transform himself at sunset into Ra, the sun god, and descend into the kingdom of the dead. There the giant snake Apophis embodying the forces of darkness and chaos is waiting for him. After a fierce struggle, Ramses II kills Apophis and returns at sunrise as king.

37

Festivals and Ceremonies

The Mysteries of Abydos

In Egypt there is a popular story that goes back to the dawn of time, when the gods still lived among the people. The story goes like this. Osiris, son of Geb, the god of earth, and Nut, the goddess of the sky, had a brother named Seth and two sisters, Isis and Nephti. Isis married Osiris and Nephti married Seth.

Osiris revealed the secrets of civilization to men and gave them the first laws, so he was made their king. This honor filled Seth with envy. Seth enticed Osiris into a trap, killed him, and buried his body in Asia.

Isis was devastated by her husband's death, but she was determined to find him. She put her own magical powers to work. After long and difficult journeys, she found her husband's body and brought it back to Egypt. But Seth spied on her, discovered where she had hidden Osiris's body, dismembered it, and scattered the pieces throughout the land.

Isis did not give up. Helped by her sister Nephti, she recovered the pieces one by one, reassembled the body and, with the help of Anubis, the jackal god, she embalmed the body, making it incorruptable. Osiris now had a spark of life and with Isis had a son named Horus who had the head of a hawk.

However, the ressurected Osiris could no longer live among people. His destiny was to reign in the underworld, in the kingdom of the dead. He chose Horus to succeed him on the throne of Egypt. Seth fiercely opposed this decision and managed to tear from Horus his far-seeing eye, or *ugiat* in Egyptian. But the sun god Ra gave the eye back to Horus. This led to a dispute that ended before a sacred court that awarded Horus the crown of the Two Kingdoms and banished Seth to govern over the desert and over foreign lands.

This story is a simplified version of *The Mysteries of Osiris*. These stories are enacted at dusk at different times of the year, in front of the temple in the sacred city of Abydos, where the god Osiris is said to be buried.

Abydos, the Heart of Egypt

Abydos is not a great city or even an important political or economic center, but it is a famous destination for pilgrimages, thanks to the tomb of Osiris and the mysteries celebrated there. It would seem, however, that long ago Abydos was not a city, but the royal cemetry of Thinis, the first capital of Egypt, which has now disappeared.

The list of the kings of Egypt is kept here, from Horus to the present day. The story goes that Sesciat, the goddess of writing, personally keeps the list up-to-date.

Trips Outside the City

Tell el-Amarna

You will not find the city of Tell el-Amarna on a map. The name has been wiped out by command of the kings who succeeded each other to the throne of Egypt over the last 70 years.

Tell el-Amarna was a great capital built halfway between Thebes and Memphis by Pharaoh Akhenaton known as "the heretic" and his wife Nefertiti. They built the city in honor of Aton whom they had proclaimed to be the "god of gods" of all Egypt. It was an ambitious project for them to make the city that we call Tell el-Amarna today, the kingdom of god on earth, and a place of universal peace and harmony.

After the deaths of Akhenaton and Nefertiti, the project was discontinued, the place was abandoned, and there was a return to the old gods and the old order. That is the reason that Tell el-Amarna, which once had more than 40,000 inhabitants, is now only a dry plain, with the ruins of a building or a tomb here and there.

The memory of the city has not, however,

THE FORMS OF THE GOD
The sun plays a central part in Egyptian religion. Known as "the Lord of all forms," which his light makes visible, Aton can assume different sacred forms. At dawn he is Khepri, the scarab, a symbol of the force of creation and being. At midday he is Ra, generating fire at the peak of his power, represented by a man with a hawk's head surmounted by a star. At sunset he is Atum, the god at the beginning and end of everything. Aton is the pure and simple disk form of the sun, the essence of all these other different forms.

completely vanished. From time to time groups of foreign diplomats stationed in Egypt obtain special permission to visit the ruins provided they are escorted by soldiers and authorized guides. Mingle with them if you can.

The trip on the Nile from Thebes to Tell el-Amarna offers unforgettable sights. Rocked by the current, you will be able to admire wide, green expanses of fields followed by small plots of cultivated land and, in the distance, steep walls of white rock sloping down into bright hills.

Amarnian Art

Rays of the sun and outstretched hands granting light and life to the pharaoh and to his chief wife. Spiritual faces, ageless, sexless bodies, establish the divine nature of the royal couple. Flowers, plants, animals, landscapes have been preserved as they originally appeared. Soft, warm colors are matched in harmony. The few traces that remain of Amarnian art are enough to fill us with wonder.

41

Trips Outside the City

The Pyramids of Giza and the Sphinx

People say they have been there forever and that the "youngest" is over 1,200 years old. A proverb has even been written about them: A man fears time, but even time fears the pyramids. Little is known about these three stone giants that seem to appear out of nowhere in the midst of the dry plain of Giza. We know they go back to the time of three pharaohs who reigned in the Ancient Kingdom—Khufu, or Cheops; Khafre, or Chephren; and Menkaure, or Mycerinus—and that there is nothing similar in the whole of the known world. We know, too, that the biggest, the pyramid of Khufu, is a mountain of square blocks of white limestone and granite, over 340 small cubits (about 490 feet) high and weighing over five million tons. It's dimensions are superhuman!

Then there is the Sphinx, the baffling Sphinx—a huge, crouching lion with the head of a man, his eyes raised to the horizon. It was carved from a hill almost 196 feet long and almost 66 feet high. For the Egyptians this monument is both the guardian of the site and the incarnation of the divine origin of the pharaonic monarchy.

The Egyptians believe that hidden forces permanently link the Sphinx with the other pyramids, making Giza a place with an extraordinary atmosphere. This is why, despite its great age, the group is subject to continuous restoration, the most recent of which began just a few years ago.

The Mystery of the Pyramids

What are the pyramids of Giza really? There are many stories about their origin. Some say they are the empty tombs of three great pharaohs. Others remind us that the real name of the necropolises of Giza is *Rosetau*, meaning "the roads to the other world, or the afterlife." These roads lead to the boundaries of the heavens, and that is where the kings are reborn in the form of immortal stars. Still others remind us that there are dozens and dozens of pyramids in Egypt, which, like the obelisks with their golden tops, are nothing more than mirrors to reflect the sun—or are even there to remind us of the hill from which the world was created. It is for you to decide!

The Missing Statue

Have you ever noticed that the Sphinx's chest looks quite empty? Well, this is another of the mysteries connected with Giza. It was believed that the Sphinx once wore a wide collar on its chest and held high between its paws the statue of a pharaoh with a hawk in flight. The hawk held the symbol of the universe in its claws. No trace of that belief remains today.

The Pharaoh's Dream

Between the feet of the Sphinx, you will notice a tall stele, or upright stone slab, made from pink granite. It goes back to the restoration carried out more than 120 years ago by Thutmose IV. On the stele there is a text that tells a story. Prince Thutmose was out hunting in the area close to the Sphinx, which was then almost completely buried by the desert sand. Thutmose fell fast asleep and dreamed that the Sphinx appeared to him and said, "Save me, my son! If you free me from the sand, I will make you king." He did what the Sphinx asked and the Sphinx, in turn, kept its promise.

Trips Outside the City

Abu Simbel

To see the two most famous temples built into rock that exist in the Egyptian Empire, you will have to sail up the Nile into the heart of Nubia. There you will marvel at the two temples dedicated to Ramses II and his chief royal wife Nefertari. The temples will suddenly appear before you, carved into the huge blocks of yellow-pink sandstone, at a bend in the river.

The temple of Nefertari appears first. She has been immortalized as Hathor, the goddess of love. Two statues of the goddess stand near the entrance to the temple. Each is more than 33 feet high and is guarded by two imposing statues of Ramses II in a standing position. The work sends a double message of love—the message of eternal love between the two sovereigns and each one's love for the region of Nubia.

Next you come before the most important temple. It is carved into a rock face almost 131 feet long and more than 85 feet high. Four colossi of Ramses II seated on a throne decorate the front of the temple. One of the four partially collapsed after an earthquake but has been left unrepaired at the request of the Pharaoh. In spite of this, the temple inspires a great sense of awe and power. Perhaps this is what the whole work aimed to

Nubia: A Divine Region
Egyptians are not particularly sympathetic toward the Nubians who are too proud and too rebellious for the Egyptians' taste. However, the Egyptians love the Nubian region for three good reasons. Nubia is a beautiful region. It is the birthplace of the god Amon; the protector of the ruling dynasty. There is gold in Nubia! *Nubia* means "land of gold," and it is the region that is, in effect, a mine for the two lands. However, it is not just a source of gold but copper and amethyst, too. For the Egyptians gold, an incorruptible metal, symbolizes the sun and the flesh of the gods.

achieve. The first name of the Pharaoh was carved in the form of a riddle on the temple face, *Usermaatra,* meaning "the powerful and cosmic influence of Ra."

Enemies overcome in battle appear as carved figures under the soles of the huge statues' sandals. This confirms Egypt's control over Nubia. People say that deep inside the temple, Ramses II is painted seated beside the three most important gods of the Two Kingdoms: Amon of Thebes, Ptah of Memphis, and Ra of Heliopolis.

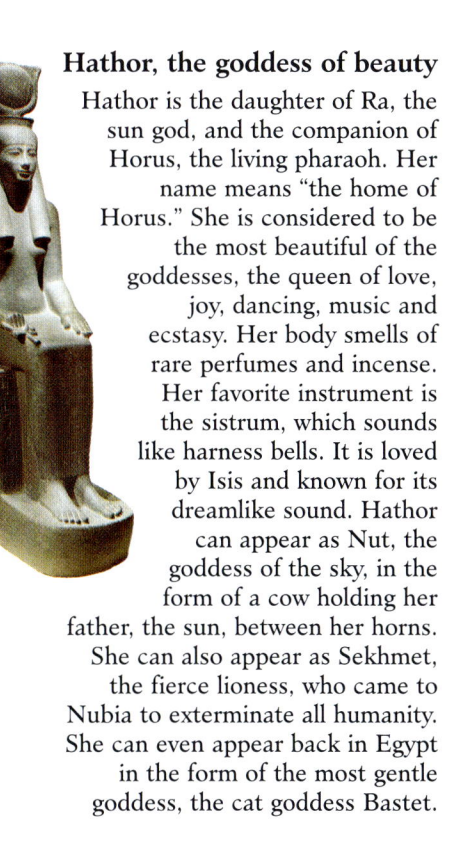

Hathor, the goddess of beauty

Hathor is the daughter of Ra, the sun god, and the companion of Horus, the living pharaoh. Her name means "the home of Horus." She is considered to be the most beautiful of the goddesses, the queen of love, joy, dancing, music and ecstasy. Her body smells of rare perfumes and incense. Her favorite instrument is the sistrum, which sounds like harness bells. It is loved by Isis and known for its dreamlike sound. Hathor can appear as Nut, the goddess of the sky, in the form of a cow holding her father, the sun, between her horns. She can also appear as Sekhmet, the fierce lioness, who came to Nubia to exterminate all humanity. She can even appear back in Egypt in the form of the most gentle goddess, the cat goddess Bastet.

The Armed Forces

The Fortress of Buhen

If you wish to understand the outstanding technical level reached by the Egyptian military architects, you have to visit the Nubian fortress of Buhen. This construction is part of a chain of 13 forts that have defended the Egyptian domination of Nubia for more than 700 years. A similar, but more recent system of defense, has been erected to the north, on the border with Asia. However, because of the continuous disorders in the area, you will not be allowed to visit there.

Over time a peaceful town with residential districts and even a market has developed near the Fortress of Buhen. That is why the presence of foreign tourists holding safe-conduct passes is tolerated. The fortress is built on a steep, rocky promontory that makes it impossible to capture from the river. The side facing the land is defended by a double set of walls and a moat. The ramparts are more than 20 small cubits high (36 feet) and 10 small cubits (18 feet) thick. Guard towers stand at regular intervals, con-

The Nine Arches
The Nubians are famous for their archery skills. That is why they make up a special corps in the Egyptian army. But this was not always the case. There was a time when the confederation of the most hostile Nubian tribes, the so-called "nine arches" caused a lot of trouble for the Egyptian army. Since that time the expression "nine arches" has been synonymous with the word enemy *in Egyptian.*

nected with each other by a grooved walkway for patrols. The walkway has double loopholes that allow archers to keep the surrounding area within their sights and under control.

The main entrance to the fortress faces the desert. It is a long, narrow corridor closed by two double gates linked by a wooden bridge. The fortress houses a permanent garrison of 300 men. Mounted messengers keep in continuous contact with the other fortresses in the chain and with Egypt itself.

SOLDIERS AND SACRED DIVISIONS!

The Egyptian army boasts of four divisions of 5,000 men each, a total of 20,000 soldiers. The divisions are named after the four main gods worshiped by the Egyptians: Amon, Ptah, Seth, and Ra. These soldiers defeated the huge Hittite army at Kadesh, in Syria. The most important temples in the Two Kingdoms have paintings commemorating the battle. Ramses II is shown leading his troops into battle seated on his battle-wagon, with the hand of Amon guiding him to victory. Whether it really was like that, we do not know. What is certain is that the Egyptian cavalry with its Nubian archers played a great part.

Egypt Today

Present-Day Egypt

More than other countries of North Africa today, Egypt is a study in contrasts. From the great cities, like Cairo, to the smallest villages, from the sophisticated city-dwellers to the simple farmers or fishers, from Coptic Christians to Islamic fundamentalists or devout Muslims, Egypt today is very different from ancient Egypt.

Cairo hums with activity and is more like a cosmopolitan city than other major African cities. But far beyond Cairo, the villages in the Upper Nile valley are extremely simple. It is strange for us to think of a hovel, equipped with a TV but no running water. Impossible, you say, but it is true. Primitive dwellings in the countryside are not an exception, even in our era. Yes, it is true that the areas along the Nile, especially within the delta are the most populated of Egypt.

Thousands of tourists visit Egypt to see the magnificent and mysterious monuments the pharaohs left behind. This ancient land will always be a fascinating place.

The Temple of Amon in Karnak

Here is the Great Temple of Amon in Karnak, Egypt. The ruins are still very impressive, but nothing remains of the houses, palaces, and gardens from ancient times. This was the largest of all Egyptian temples. It is like an important historical document in stone, showing many events in the Egyptian empire in both carvings and hieroglyphics on the towers and pillars.

The second photograph of the Great Temple is the immense pillared hall built by Ramses I.

The Temple at Luxor

This is how the Temple at Luxor on the banks of the Nile River looks today. The temple was a palace where the God lived, surrounded by his priests and servants. King Amenhotep III of the 18th Dynasty built this temple.

48

Market

This photograph shows a very unusual market. Here camels are bought and sold! This is the camel market at Imbabah, a suburb of Cairo, the capital city of Egypt. Egyptians gather each day in this part of the city to sell and buy camels that have been brought from Sudan by dealers.

The smaller picture is of the vegetable market stand in Luxor. It is a typical scene in Arab countries. The customers bargain when they do their shopping. Bargaining for the lowest price is a common practice.

The Temple of Hatshepsut (18th Dynasty)

This is the burial temple of Queen Hatshepsut. Set against the cliff of Deir el-Bahari, it is quite dramatic. The Ancient Egyptians believed the goddess, who was the guardian of the necropolis, lived there. The famous reliefs tell the story of the the miraculous birth of this queen. The combination of the human-made design and the cliff—one echoing the other—heightens the impact of the structure.

Colossi of Memnon

If you want to feel dwarfed, go and stand near the Colossi of Memnon! The name of Memnon, a hero in Greek mythology and king of the Ethiopians, was linked to the colossal stone statues erected by the Pharaoh Amenhotep III near Thebes. Now only two statues, some 70-feet tall, remain. The one standing farther north was partially destroyed by an earthquake in 27 B.C. Each morning when the rays of the rising sun struck the statue, those nearby could hear musical sounds like plucking of a harp string. In 170 A.D., a Roman emperor ordered the statue be restored. Since then, the sounds ceased. The scientific explanation is that they were caused by air passing through the pores of the stone, because of the change of temperature at sunrise.

Egypt Today

Boats on the Nile

The Nile River today is lined with modern office buildings that contrast sharply with the ancient style of the feluccas, the sailing boats that are still seen on the river. The feluccas have a distinctive triangular sail on a diagonally sloping mast. This narrow vessel is still used to carry building materials like stones, bricks, or sand, or even small animals like goats.

The Great Sphinx and Pyramids of Giza

This photograph shows the Great Sphinx and the Pyramid of Menkaure in Giza, Egypt. There are two other pyramids on the site, those of the Pharaohs Khufu and Khafre. These three pyramids together are considered the greatest in all Egypt.

The pyramids in Ancient Egypt were all built as tombs for the pharaohs and their queens. The Pyramids of Giza were built for pharaohs of the Fourth Dynasty. The Ancient Egyptians believed the form of the pyramid helped the dead pharaoh to climb up to the heavens to reunite with the sun. For years the favorite pastime of tourists to Giza was to climb up to the summit of the pyramids. This was an extremely dangerous activity and is strictly forbidden now. The pyramid of Khufu or Kheops is the only one of the Seven Wonders of the Ancient World that has survived more or less intact to the present.

We find the world-famous form of the Great Sphinx on the same site as the three pyramids of Giza. It was almost certainly carved from a rocky spur, the shape of which probably resembled the final shape of the monument. The Great Sphinx was created almost 25 centuries before our time. In mythology a sphinx is a creature with a lion's body and a human head. The Great Sphinx in Giza was the colossal figure of the Pharaoh Khafre, fourth king of the Fourth Dynasty and was supposed to be both the guardian and symbol of royalty. It has long suffered from the effects of erosion and the slow upward movement of underground water.

Abu Simbel

Imagine moving two enormous Ancient Egyptian temples, stone by stone to another site, 175 miles from the original one. This was the huge undertaking that attracted worldwide attention when the two Abu Simbel Temples erected by Pharaoh Ramses II were threatened with flooding by the waters from the Aswan High Dam. In 1959, Egypt appealed to UNESCO to help save these Nubian monuments, relics of the oldest human civilization. Salvage operations to move the temples started in 1963 and cost around $36 million. The Abu Simbel temples were relocated to a plateau where yearly thousands of visitors continue to marvel at their majesty. The Aswan High Dam, completed in 1970, has allowed the annual Nile flood to be controlled for the first time in history.

The large photograph shows the Greater Abu Simbel Temple built by Ramses II, and dedicated to the sun god Ra-Harakhte. The second photograph shows the Smaller Temple that was dedicated by Ramses II to his beautiful wife.

Of all the temples and relics built by the Pharaoh Ramses II the first and largest of the two temples is the most striking. Its huge facade is guarded by four 65-foot high statues of Ramses II. High on the facade is a row of carved, smiling baboons. On the doorway of the temple is a wonderful inscription of the king's name: Ser-Ma'at-Ra. Beyond the entrance, is the Great Hall of Pillars, where eight pillars show the deified Ramses II in the shape of Osiris. Next comes a smaller hall, the hall of the nobles, which contains four square pillars. Deep within the temple you will pass into the holiest of places where you will see four statues: Ra-Harakhte, Ptah, Amun-Ra, and King Ramses II himself. The sun shines directly into this holiest place only two days a year: on February 21st, the date of the king's birthday, and October 22nd, the date of his coronation.

Some Important Dates

Important Facts

Before Dynasties • Between the sixth and the fourth millenium B.C., numerous agricultural settlements grew up in the Nile Delta and the Nile Valley. These gave rise to several regional principalities in both the region of Lower Egypt to the north and Upper Egypt to the south.

Early Dynastic Period • Around 3200 B.C., King Menes of Upper Egypt unified the country and founded the First Dynasty of the pharaohs, with its capital in Thinis, in the south. Under the Second Dynasty the center of the kingdom moved north, to Memphis, another city founded by Menes.

The Ancient Kingdom • This period covers five centuries, from the Third Dynasty to the Sixth Dynasty (around 2700-2200 B.C.). This was the golden period of Egypt under the pharaohs, the age of the great pyramids, begun by King Djoser with the Step Pyramid at Saqqara and reaching its height around 2500 B.C., with the Sphinx and the pyramids built in Giza by Khufu, Khafre, and Menkaure. The Ancient Kingdom ended with Pepy I. He reigned for more than 90 years, a time when the central authority of the state was weakened.

First Intermediate Period • For roughly a century and a half (Seventh Dynasty to Eleventh Dynasty), a period followed when weak rulers, who were strongly influenced by local princes, reigned.

The Middle Kingdom • Theban King Montuhotep II of the Eleventh Dynasty restored unity to the nation in 2064 B.C. He also made Thebes the new capital of the Two Kingdoms. The Middle Kingdom reached the height of its importance during the Twelfth Dynasty (1994-1797 B.C.). This is considered the classical period of the civilizations of the pharaohs.

The country's wealth rose because of the use of tillage and plowing in agriculture and the increase in the amount of land cultivated. The foundations of the empire were laid with Egyptian territorial expansion into Nubia and the Middle East.

Second Intermediate Period • At the end of the Twelfth Dynasty came a period of disorder. The Hyksos, invaders from Palestine, seized the opportunity to subdue the north and center of Egypt (Fifteenth Dynasty and Sixteenth Dynasty, 1660-1543 B.C.). The nation's recovery led by the Theban princes resulted in the expulsion of the Hyksos and the reunification of the Two Kingdoms.

The New Kingdom • This period lasted four and a half centuries, from the Eighteenth Dynasty to the Twentieth Dynasty (1543-1078 B.C.). It was the time of greatest splendor in Egyptian history and is often referred to as the Imperial, or Renaissance, period. The Eighteenth Dynasty counts the highest number of famous monarchs: the Pharaoh Queen Hatshepsut; Thutmose III, Amenophis III, who made Egypt a great military and economic power; Akhenaton known as "the heretic," and the boy-king Tutankhamen. But the most famous pharaoh of all belongs to the Nineteenth Dynasty—Ramses II, the victor of the Battle of Kadesh. The final prominent personality in the New Kingdom is Ramses III, who at the end of the twelfth century B.C., drove back the attempt to invade Egypt by the "peoples from the sea," possibly the Philistines and the Sicilians.

Third Intermediate Period • Egypt was divided again between the 11th and 8th centuries B.C., first under the kings of Tanis, in the Delta, then under the Libyan kings.

The Late Period • The Nubian Pharaoh Piankhi (Twenty-fifth Dynasty) reunified the Two Kingdoms in 715 B.C., but the nation's independence was already in jeopardy. The Assyrians occupied Egypt between 668 and 654 B.C., but were driven back by the Egyptian kings of Sais (Twenty-sixth Dynasty). In 525 B.C., the Egyptians were overthrown by the Persians. The three final Egyptian dynasties survived for a little more than half a century. A second Persian occupation in 341 B.C., followed by Alexander the Great's conquest of Macedonia in 332 B.C., marked the end of the period of the pharaohs' rule in Egypt.

Glossary

ankh (AHNK) Hieroglyphic shaped like a cross with a loop at the top, symbolizing eternal life

cataract Rough water caused by the presence of rocks along the course of the Nile River

deben A unit of value used as a basis for commerce

dynasty A series of rulers from the same royal family or the period of their rule

ged A pillar with three horizontal bars, symbolizing stability and duration

henti Period of 120 years, at the end of which a whole month is added to the Egyptian civil year to synchronize it with the astronomical year

hierogamia The sacred rite during which the pharaoh and his chief wife commemorate the union of the gods they both represent

hieroglyphics (HIGH row GLIFF icks) The most ancient Egyptian system of writing using picture symbols. It is based on special signs and images that may represent words, sounds, or symbols. A kind of picture writing: used for official inscriptions on monuments

hypostyle A room, hall, or part of a temple, the ceiling of which is held up by rows of pillars or columns

ka Essence or vital force of a person or the creative force of a god

khol Dark eye shadow used to make up the eyes

Ma'at A combination of the concepts of truth, justice, and harmony, personified by the goddess of the same name

natron (NAY trahn) Natural sodium salts found in soil and used during the process of embalming mummies

obelisk (AHB uh lihsk) A four-sided pillar with a top shaped like a pyramid

papyrus (puh PIE rus) A tall reed that grows in the Nile Valley, the spongy center part of which was used to make a paperlike substance

pharaoh (FAY row) Title given to the Egyptian kings starting with Tutmosis III, derived from the name of the royal palace meaning "great house"

sanctuary Area of an Egyptian temple where a god's statue was kept, and where the priests performed the daily ritual to the god

scribe Professional writer usually working for the state and the temples

senet Egyptian board game similar to checkers

shaduf Lever method of raising water from a lower to a higher level for irrigation

spelt A wheat with lax spikes and two red kernels

ugiat Eye of Horus, the hawk god, symbolizing energy and magical protection

usciabti Statuettes believed to have magical powers, destined to serve the dead person in the afterlife

vizier (vih ZIHR) Most important state dignitary after the pharaoh

Further Reading

Aldred, Cyril. *Tutankhamun.* Bellerophon Books, 1978.

Clare, John D., ed. *Pyramids of Ancient Egypt.* (Living History series). Harcourt, 1992.

Conway, Lorraine. *Ancient Egypt.* (Gifted Learning series). Good Apple, 1987.

Crosher, Judith. *Technology in the Time of Ancient Egypt.* Raintree Steck-Vaughn, 1998.

Diamond, Arthur. *Egypt: Gift of the Nile.* Silver Burdett Press, 1992.

Holmes, Burton. *Egypt.* (World 100 Years Ago series). Chelsea House, 1999.

Ikram, Salima. *Pharaohs.* (In Ancient Egypt series). Hoopoe Books, 1997.

Katan, Norma J., and Mintz, Barbara. *Heiroglyphs: The Writing of Ancient Egypt.* Simon and Schuster, 1981.

Malam, John. *Ancient Egypt.* (Remains to Be Seen series). Trafalgar, 1998.

McNeil, Sarah, and Howarth, Sarah. *Ancient Egyptian People.* (People and Places series). Millbrook Press, 1997.

Morley, Jacqueline. *How Would You Survive As an Ancient Egyptian?* (How Would You Survive? Series). Watts, 1996.

Parker, Jane. *Pyramids and Temples.* (Superstructures series). Raintree Steck-Vaughn, 1997.

Payne, Elizabeth. *Pharaohs of Ancient Egypt.* (Landmark Books series). Knopf, 1998.

Shields, Charles. *Life in Ancient Egypt.* (Way People Live series). Lucent Books, 1997.

Steiner, Barbara. *Mummy.* Scholastic Inc., 1995.

Index

Abu Simbel, 51
Abydos, 38–39
Achilles, 20
addresses, 9
afterlife, 23, 27, 33, 35, 37, 43
Akhenaton, 40, 52
Amenhotep III, 20, 49
Amenophis III, 52
Amon, 12–14, 31, 34, 35, 44, 45, 47, 48
Amonet, 14
amulets, 19, 37
ankh, 33
Anubis, 21, 38
Apophis, 37
archery, 46
armed forces, 46–47
art and architecture, 20–23, 41
artists, 26, 27
astronomy, 18
Aswan, 30
Aton, 40
authorizations, 8
awards ceremonies, 16, 17

baboons, 28
bartering, 8
Bastet, 25, 45
beer, 10
"black earth," 5
blue, 9
boats, 35
braids, 11
bread, 10
Buhen, 5, 46–47
bull's tail, 36
burial places, 6

calendars, 11, 18
cat goddess, 25, 45
cats, 25
cemetery, 39
ceremony of opening the mouth, 27
charms, 19
Cheops, 42
Chephren, 42
children, 11
climate, 9

clocks, 11
clothing, 9
colossi, 44
Colossi of Memnon, 20–21, 49
craftsmen, 26, 33
creation, 12, 33
crimes, 8
crowns, 17, 36
currency, 8

dance, 25
deben, 8
Deir el-Bahari, 9, 22–23, 49
Deir el-Medina, 26–27
diplomatic corps, 32
divine law, 8
doctors, 9, 22
dress, 9
dynastic periods, 52

East Thebes, 6, 24
Egypt (name), 33
Elephantine, 30–31
epagomeni, 29

farmers, 28–29
feathers, 33
Festival of Opet, 34–35
festival of the bull's tail, 36
festivals and ceremonies, 8, 10, 32–39
Fields of Ialu, 23
flooding (Nile), 4, 9, 14, 15, 29, 31
food, 8, 10
fortress of Buhen, 46–47
funeral rites, 27
funeral temples, 20–21

gardens, 24
Geb, 38
ged, 36
gestures, 9
Giza, 42–43, 50
gods and goddesses, 8, 11, 13, 14, 19, 22, 25, 29, 31, 33–40, 44, 45
gold, 44
government, 14

Hapi, 4, 5, 12
Hathor, 14, 37, 44, 45
Hatshepsut, 22, 23, 49, 52
heaven, 23
hierarchies, 11
hierogami, 14
hieroglyphics, 19
holidays, 10, 34
Horus, 38, 39, 45
houses, 24–25, 28–29
Houses of Life, 9, 18–19
hygiene, 11
Hyksos, 52
hypostyle, 12

ibises, 29
incense tree, 22
Isis, 38, 45

ka, 15
Karnak, 6, 12, 13, 24, 34, 35
Khafre (Chephren), 42, 50, 52
Khebait dancers, 25
Khepri, 40
Khnum, 31
Khonsu, 13, 34, 35
Khufu (Cheops), 42, 52
kingdoms, 52
Kjoser, 52

land ownership, 28
laws, 8, 33, 38
learning centers, 18
libraries, 18
lodging, 8
loggia, 17
Lower Egypt, 36, 52
Luxor, 6, 14, 24, 34, 48

Ma'at, 8, 11, 14, 33
magic, 9, 11, 18, 19
makeup, 9
map of Egypt, 4–5
markets, 10, 30–31
measurement, 10, 31
medicine, 9
Mediterranean Sea, 9
Memnon, 20
Memphis, 32–33, 52

55

Menes, 33, 52
Menkaure (Mycerinus), 42, 52
Mennefer, 33
Merseger, 22
money, 8
Montuhotep II, 52
monuments, 8, 42
mummies, 27
music, 25
Mut, 13, 14, 34, 35
Mycerinus, 42
The Mysteries of Osiris, 38

necropolises, 6, 22, 26, 43
Nefertiti, 40, 44
neighborhoods, 14, 24–29
Nephti, 38
Nile River, 4–5, 9
nilometer, 31
"nine arches," 46
nobility, 6, 11
Nubia, 44–46, 52
Nubians, 10, 51
Nut, 45

obelisks, 30, 43
Old City, 12–18
Opet, 34
oracles, 35
Osiris, 38, 39

palaces, 10, 16–17
Pepy I, 52
perfume, 13
pharaohs, 6, 7, 9, 11, 14, 17, 20–22, 26, 32, 33, 35, 36, 42, 45, 50, 51, 52
Piankhi, 52
Pi Ramesse, 36–37
police, 8, 9
portraits, 27
potters, 31
priests, 11, 21, 22, 31
Ptah, 33, 45, 47
publishing, 18
Punt, 22
pyramids, 43, 52
pyramids of Giza, 42–43

Ra, 13, 25, 35, 37, 40, 45, 47
Ramses II, 11, 16, 20, 36–37, 44, 45, 47, 52
Ramses III, 52
reanimation, 27
receptions, 24–25
religion, 11, 40
Rosetau, 43
royal families, 6
Royal Jubilee at Pi Ramesse, 36–37
Royal Palace of Ramses II, 16–18
royal residences, 8

sacred boat, 35
sacred lake, 12
sacred places, 8
sacred rites, 36
sacred symbols, 19
sanki, 27
sarcophagi, 27
scarabs, 19, 40
school, 18
scribes, 8, 9
Sekhmet, 14, 29, 45
senet, 8
Senmut, 22
Sesciat, 39
Seth, 38, 47
shaduf, 28
ships, 34, 35
shopping, 10
Sinai, 37
slaves, 11
soldiers, 47
souls, 15, 35
Sphinx, 42–43, 50, 52
sphinxes, 12, 23
stars, 43
statues, 27, 34, 35, 43, 44
stele, 43
Step Pyramid, 52
sun, 40, 44

Tauri, 5
taxes, 28, 30

teaching, 18
Tell el-Amarna, 40–41
Temple of Amon, 6, 7, 12–14, 18, 35
Temple of Ka Ptah, 33
Temple of Karnak, 14
temples, 6–8, 10, 20–22, 44–45, 47
Theban Triad, 13, 34
Thebes, 6–7, 9, 20, 31, 52
Thinis, 39
Thoth, 19, 29
Thutmose III, 52
Thutmose IV, 43
time, 11
tombs, 19, 43
toys, 11
trade, 8
travel, 4
tribute at Memphis, 32–33
Turquoise City, 37
Tutankhamen, 52
Two Kingdoms, 5, 7, 52

ugiat, 38
underworld, 37, 38
Upper Egypt, 14, 30, 36, 52
usciabti, 27
Usermaatra, 45

Valley of the Kings, 6, 7, 22
Valley of the Queens, 6
Vast Green Water, 5
villas, 24
vizier, 32, 33

wealthy classes, 9, 10, 24–25
weighing scales of the Two Kingdoms, 33
weights, 8, 10
Western Peak, 22
West Thebes, 6, 16, 20, 21
women, 11
working-class districts, 26–29